Prison Segmentation

for

Lifer Purpose Plans

Rev. Mike Wanner

Table Of Content

Introduction

Life is not comfortable for any of us, and we all have our challenges. Prisoners incarcerated for life have fewer options and a lot of time.

I hope this book offers some ideas for contemplation and peace.

Reverend Mike

1 - Why I am Writing This Book

I have been writing a series of books about possibilities for prisons, prison staff and others who are associated with the prison community.

The one area of the system that seems like an utterly unsolvable situation is the future for lifers, the prisoners who have been designated never to be able to exit prison. As I continue to write about possibilities that could be created as potentials for prisoners, anything positive for lifers seemed camouflaged from view.

While everything that I was writing for other prisoners might be a stretch for all readers, I knew this book would be even more difficult to explain in a way that can be understood. I felt, however, that it needed to be written.

As we all go along in our existence, life can get boring. Sometimes, ideas will be presented that Pearce the boredom and stimulate thought about people and ideas that have never before had any appeal.

Boredom for lifers might be enough to allow some ideas that can change their perspective. It is never to late to review the life you have lived and the potential for future days.

You Can open your mind enough to allow introspection, inspiration, and reinitiation and then how about a reality check and a substitution plan. Nobody ever gets all s/he wants all the time, but deliberate action, planning, prayer, and positivity can produce options that can bring some peace.

2 - Determination Of Interest

Lifers would have to at some point know enough about the segmentation efforts to express an interest in participation. They could hear about successes and failures, so they could think about what might be right for them.

If there was any interest in the segmentation process, the prisoner with a life sentence would have to apply for the program like everybody else. Each prison may have different rules so it may work out that some may get an opportunity and some may not, especially early on.

After determining that one is interested, further research about the availability and application criteria would be needed to determine the next steps. Nothing can be taken for granted.

Besides hard work, persistence is a significant determinant. There will be complications, and stick-to-it determination will be an excellent tool to continue using until success becomes history.

When triumph is accomplished, new goals will be the motivation that shares your hard work to further the lives that come after you. But Before all that, you would need to know what you would like to participate in during segmentation.

3 - What do You Want To Do?

You can get creative now and play with possibilities that can change prison dynamics, help the system and help many more people in the future. Please try to develop concepts that can fragment the status quo so that it can be reassembled into new configurations that you have left your imprint on.

The usual reaction to the question "What do You Want To Do?" is usually something like " I don't Know." The surprise is that you do not need to know, you can just create an answer out of thin air that captures the reality of possibilities that you would like to create.

Next step would be to capture what you dreamt up in a way that you can share. After that, share your record of all that developed out of your casual approach.

Congratulations because you have drafted something that has a raw potential for something that can work eventually. You will have arrived at a point of creativity that can be later polished into something that will be palatable to many people.

Please know that proposals never finish in the original format, so there is little value in trying for perfection at the outset. Keep the content you create and give it a short time to speak to you about what to do next.

4 - Hell Then, Now, and What's Next?

Have you learned anything of value in your life that might give you pause to reassess aspects of the things that you see from your viewing position?

Have you found solace lately in the opportunities that present themselves for your consideration?

Have you understood man's inhumanity to man and why it happens and who is the victim?

Would you like to find some answers from a personal power perspective?

If you could, would you take the initiative to make up to people you might have wronged?

Have you been able to find forgiveness for others who may have obstructed your positive perspectives for your life or did not support your analysis truthfully?

Have you been able to find forgiveness for yourself and everything that did or did not do?

Do you feel the need to develop a plan for your future?
Might the ideal plan be more natural to process if you were able to plan for others with more options so that you could live vicariously through them while you are bringing peace, tranquility, and purpose to the life that you are living?

The vibrancy of their possibilities can bring a kind of virtual reality purpose to yours.

Many lifers have stepped down to a low vibration that does not support joy and life well. As you step up your vibration, you become a higher vibration being who is better able to vibrate at frequencies that are more compatible with manifesting more positive frequencies for manifestation.

Also as time goes on, you may just accumulate a large group of supporters who live outside the walls and could initiate plans to benefit you. Part of your time while those you mentor are still in prison may be about aligning interests, so they can have ideas that may help the whole jail community more as time progress.

A principle of life is that "What goes around come around(Anon)." so if you never tried it before, consider giving it a go. The worst case scenario is that every day will be less internally focussed.

5 - Prisoner Advocates

Seniority is an indication of wisdom and perspective.
Your familiarity with the building and the rules and the staff
can help you to help others to understand how to navigate the
tough times.

Lifers could retitle themselves "Prisoner Advocates,"
"Permanent Residents" or a term or series of phrases that reflect
their resident station with a positive habitational characteristic.

Prisoners advocates who wish to keep the respect and title will
best solidify their position by statesmanship and practicality. It
is essential for advocates to be able to see the highest good for
all parties in all things at all times.

There are 15 segment books, and each of those topics could be
evaluated for possible inclusion in your home prison.

The segments proposed are:
1. Prison Segmentation For Safety, And Sanity,
   Security, Peace, and Space
2. Prison Segmentation For Security
3. Prison Segmentation For Mental peace
4. Prison Segmentation For Joint Ventures
5. Prison Segmentation For Startup
6. Prison Segmentation For Your Rehabilitation: R U
   Ready?
7. Prison Segmentation For Family Villages

6 - Why Try?

In Youth, and many lifers were convicted in theirs, we/you/they may not fully understand all the forces and opportunities that are available to citizens of a free society. You may not even be aware of all the rights that you have.

Prison is somewhat of a barrier to information because the right information at the right time in the right way applied by the right people may be effectuated to unlock potentials that have been secured away. While information may be available to prisoners, please note the use of the words above and the importance thereof – the right information, the right time, the right way and the right people.

If a combination is not explicitly applied right then, the lock may remain closed.

Depending on the many variables of each particular prisoner's circumstances, planning and application are crucial to success. The more access that you can have to free citizens and authoritative information, the more likely you may be to succeed.

In Chapter 7 , I will share a story from the bible about what Jesus said about the Prodigal Son. I hope it impresses upon Readers about the welcome that may be available for you.

In Chapter 8, I will share a reference to a movie and then a message about purpose from the channelings the Angel Raphael Speaks series.

7 - Love From Above

There is never a time where God gives up on anyone. Your journey in life and prison may have been extremely unpleasant, and you may think that you have reached a state of despair.

You may well see chaos as your reality because it is right for you at the moment that you are living in the hell that is now in the house that you live. Moments pass and so can chaos.

Have you allowed God to walk with you and feel your emotional reality? In a book titled the Bible (King James Version Luke 15:11-24) Jesus Christ told The Parable of the Lost Son.

Jesus continued: "...A certain Man had two sons:

And the younger of them said to his father, Father, give me the portion of goods that falleth to me.
And he divided unto them his living.

And not many days after the younger son gathered all together, and took his journey into a far country, and there wasted his substance with riotous living.

And when he had spent all, there arose a mighty famine in that land; and he began to be in want.

And he went and joined himself to a citizen of that country; and he sent him into his fields to feed swine.

And he would fain have filled his belly with the husks that the swine did eat: and no man gave unto him.

And when he came to himself, he said, How many hired servants of my father's have bread enough and to spare, and I perish with hunger!

I will arise and go to my father, and will say unto him, Father, I have sinned against heaven, and before thee.

And am no more worthy to be called thy son: make me as one of thy hired servants.

And he arose, and came to his father. But when he was yet a great way off, his father saw him, and had compassion, and ran, and fell on his neck and kissed him.

And the son said unto him, Father, I have sinned against heaven, and in thy sight, and am no more worthy to be called thy son.

But the father said to his servants, Bring forth the best robe, and put it on him: and put a ring on his hand, and shoes on his feet:

And bring hither the fatted calf, and kill it; and let us eat, and be merry:

For this my son was dead, and is alive again: he was lost, and is found. And they began to be merry."

Consider Yourself For Just A Minute as The Lost Child of The God Most High

8 - Image Of Possibility

The *Dirty Dozen* movie conjures up a lot of images about the human dynamics of the incarcerated. The idea aligns with the messages of Angel Raphael.

Purpose is the one thing that can move people towards the impossible. I share the Prison Rehabilitation message from the message set 10 in the Angel Raphael Speaks Series a lot.

I share the message next because it is spot-on in possibility but unfortunately challenging to consider. I hope the ideas that follow in this book can help frame a purpose that can be embraced.

"Prison Rehabilitation

The answer to prison rehabilitation is purpose. While some institutions may have initiated programs to engage their residents, the feeling of a purposeful life brings a new reality to the incarcerated.

Purposes worth considering will be ones that work for the incarcerated as well as the society which actually pays the bills. Unique characteristics to include would be the creation of a feeling of accomplishment generated by prisoner effort and drastic cost savings for the institution.

The real loss to prisons is wasted time, no productivity and no graciousness of interactive genius. If invited, the right use of time can provide different results than now seen.

There is no profit to society when cruelness is applied to the control of citizens. There may be temporary security, but that comes at a significant price to the potential of all.

The best way to learn about what is possible is to listen to the troubled stories of the incarcerated people. Their genius can be tapped by mining information about how to fill the gap that they slipped in to so that newer walkers on their path can find the hole filled by their charity of sharing their pain as a love patch to the sinkholes of society.

The answers through this channel are coming differently than most could conceive and that is because neither you nor I have a job whose agenda has its own needs.

You ask to imagine how much can be cut from prison costs to maintain security, improve lives, create new industry and improve the focus, flavor, and flair of American life and you dowsed for an answer. You got 47% reduction, and you questioned your dowsing. Your questioning is wise because there is a vast industry that has roots in the status quo.

While that is true, your answer has potential that will serve the ones that would resist the initiatives that flow from the message. Their positions are survivable as is for a time unknown but their openness to change can also serve their security.

The change will happen even if they choose to use their money to resist the inevitable avalanche of change. Their opportunities are paramount in the areas of personal safety for all and the possibility to create new meaningful arrangements that are self-sustaining for all levels of the resident base and those employed in the industry.   ARS 10

9 - Background Of Law Changes For Juvenile Lifers

In 2012, the United States Supreme Court held in Miller v. Alabama that it is unconstitutional to sentence a juvenile offender to mandatory life-without-parole. The Miller Court did not determine if the decision should be applied retroactively and left that question to the states.

January 2016, however, the United States Supreme Court held in Montgomery v. Louisiana that Miller should, in fact, be applied retroactively and should, therefore, apply to cases decided prior to the 2012 ruling. In practical terms, this means that juvenile offenders previously sentenced to mandatory life-without-parole can seek to resentence by the trial court.

Progress In Pennsylvania News

Based on the changes above, the Pennsylvania Department of Corrections reported as of December 17, 2017; they identified that the changes applied to 518 candidates and as of that date the progress was that:
>   95 were released
>   197 were resentenced
>   3 passed away

Progress In Your Local News

Check for yourself and your friends and see what is applicable in your jurisdiction.

10 - Sentence Commutations

Sentence commutations and pardons are still possible. President Trump in his short term so far has done both.

Commutations and pardons require work, and no one can expect to get one without proving that they are worthy. The concept of fairness by itself will not likely rise to the standard of proof that would be required to obtain either.

President Obama granted more commutations than any other United States President. The total is actually more than the past prior dozen presidents combined.

President Obama has granted mercy and declared executive clemency for 1,927 recipients. The total included 1,715 commutations {including 504 life sentenced prisoners} who will get a second chance and 212 pardons.

While rare still, the effort may be worth the investment in time and also the hope that the effort might bring. Hope has enormous power to motivate and keep people on track for all that might someday be possible.

Being hopeful and confident will be kinder to the body of the one who keeps the faith in God and God's blessing for even if nothing changes in the real world, belief will improve the quality of the believer's days and weeks and months. You attract what you focus on, and faith is fantastic.

11 - Compassionate Release

While not likely something that you wish to consider, it can help your mood each day to have a purpose. If you may someday age and we all will, you may qualify later for that kind of consideration.

Get ready now by documenting everything that will be needed by anyone that would consider that for you whenever it might be required. While you are alert and oriented, you can do all the analysis of all the qualifications and the history that will contribute to the decision.

Only you will have some of the information that may sway the authorities so take some time and polish pieces of your profile in the exact format that might be required later. Do not procrastinate as unforeseen events could trigger unexpected opportunities to further your path to freedom.

You may not know that the news has a lot about prisons and the conditions therein. It could occur that the judicial system might apply pressure to the prison authorities to reduce the occupancy of facilities.

If mandatory releases occur, you may exit during freedom opportunities that are totally unexpected and find yourself with new opportunities for your remaining days. Deliberate preparation could set you up to be documented, packed, and ready to go when the freedom train blows the whistle and says All Aboard the Exit Express.

12 - Segment Development

It is difficult to imagine the congestion in many prisons and Segmentation ideas have been shared in an effort to reorder the way that prisoners are moved throughout the facilities.

Every prison will have their own priorities according to the laws of the governing authorities, and they will vary from region to region. The goal of segmentation is to spread people out around the clock, and while that may seem awkward, nothing could be more awkward than some of the pictures of the congestion that you can see online.

The use of a twenty-four-hour prisoner space utilization can develop many opportunities that will show up as new freedoms of choice.

I invite each lifer to play with the concept after they have done their homework on what might be done where you are. Please use your knowledge of prison life to outline problems and then plan programs to remedy the situation.

I have offered many ideas, but your residence and terms of occupancy make you an expert, and your impact possibilities are fantastic. Please dream, analyze and share about the things that bother you most about prison life and then reframe the ideas in a way that offers everybody the opportunity to hear the views without needing to feel that they are the blame for the way things are at the time they read your opinions.

13 - A Big Gift to the Country

There seems to be a significant event on the path to prison that makes persons stopped by the police react in ways which many times can result in a triggering reactiveness that can predispose negative consequences.

The setting of the stage of complexity may be long established in time before events happen. I am cautious with my words because I have heard individuals with different group dynamics express the intensity of their predispositions.

While people have the right to feel the way they think, the act of carrying intensity can be dangerous to people who might agree with them and also those who might not.

Disagreements happen quickly, and consequences can be activated within the blink of an eye, and the results can likely be irreparable.

The country needs leadership to vulnerable communities and the authorities on how to interact with each other so that each can incrementally signal their willingness to cooperate without indicating a void of power and personal authority.

This may sound like a simple thing, but there is an issue that is unspoken that hides cooperative willingness and broadcasts defiance which is enormously infuriating to all parties.

I want to warn all and apologize to all that this is a significant issue that needs help. Lifers may be the only ones who have enough authority in both camps to create real change.

14 - Rejecting Strangers

Part of the problem discussed in the last chapter may be the rejection experienced but not verbalized. Reactiveness may be happening before either party even realizes that they have communicated eye daggers which sting. An earlier Article follows.

"Caution To Not Reject People You Do Not Know"
{From Chapter 7 of *Surviving Hate And Vulnerability In America Now!*}

The reactions between individuals are much more complicated than many may think. You may not know you are rejecting someone until you see their response to what you did not say.

The Gaze of Negativity

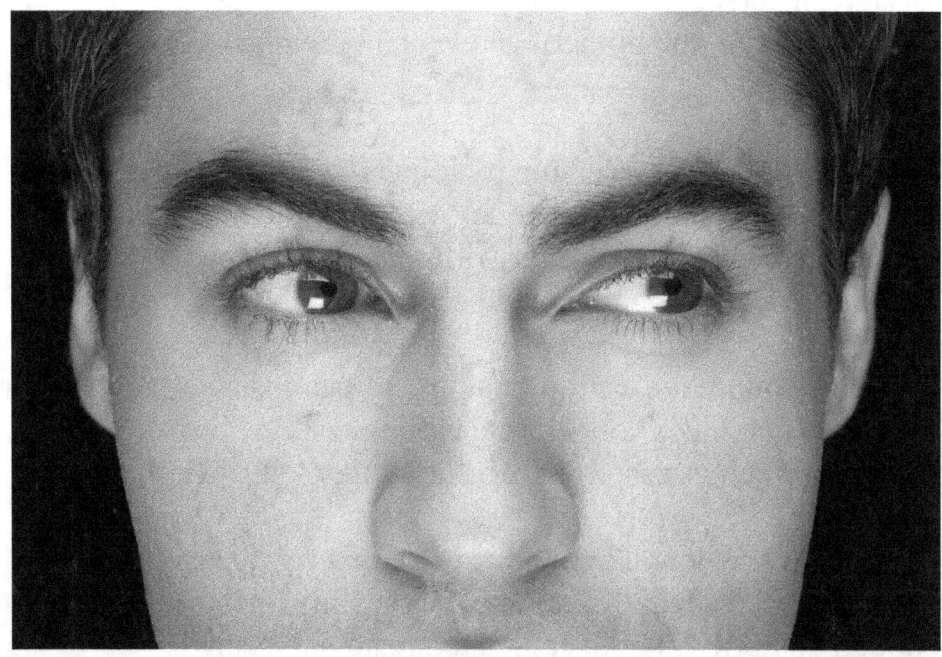

Consider a perspective I share that may not be defendable by scientific analysis but may be understood by those who try. There can be a reactive triggering within people that can influence the outcome before a word is spoken.

How many times have you heard people say that as soon as they saw something, they knew this was going to be challenging, etc. Below the surface is a pattern of experience that can taint the energy between people who do not know each other and have not spoken a single word to one another.

I call it the gaze of rejection and being aware of it can help you to avoid damage to potential interactions when meeting new people.

I hope that sharing this idea allows us all to know our own vulnerability that could signal a warning for us. There is a psychological concept called pattern interrupts that could be implemented by those who are aware.

At the least, pattern interrupts could signal some of us to be on our best behavior during challenging times and good practice can save a lot of agony and grief. We can diffuse situations by armoring ourselves with wisdom instead of weapons.

Please indulge me a little and see if you cannot remember a situation where you felt this personally. Perhaps, you were talking to a close friend about your last date, and your parent came into the room, and the conversation abruptly stopped.

You could have felt it, or your parents could have. Either way, the look hurts a lot whichever side of the issue you are on.

15 - Wrap Up

God pays attention. The Angels are listening. There is a lot that is right with the world but people in prison and outside it, do not always realize the power that they have.

Henry Ford once said in "The Reader's Digest" that "Whether you believe you can do a thing or not, you are right." I encourage you to believe you can still do a lot and I share a personal story below.

One Idea Of Possibility

I delight in telling the story of my niece to many people. It precedes the idea of "I think I can." It is the concept of I might be able to after all.

I am blessed to have a couple of delightful nieces, and they are like many of us in that they have had their challenges. My oldest niece is now a Nurse Practitioner with a Pediatric Specialty.

Earlier on in her life, her potential was not so clear to her as she graduated high school with very few career possibilities in mind. Like so many children her parents had divorced, and this left a shadow of confusion over the path of her life.

She was not thinking like the let's go to college crowd but more like the let's find a job and get to work thinkers. Then she talked about her future with my mother, and her concept of the future shifted.

She did not know nor did any of us in the family that my mother had been making steady deposits towards her education. I never knew the amount that was available nor is that important.

The information for my niece was tremendous as it launched a concept of possibility that shifted everything. Suddenly, my nieces' outlook on life was enhanced, and she thought that her life could be more and that her grandmother cared enough to help make that possible.

The idea that there was possibility grabbed hold of her mind and rekindled her dreams. She started to pursue optimistic ideas and succeeded.

The potential led to a higher blessing as her chosen career field nursing was understaffed, and there were incentive programs for possible students. The plan she chose was across the river in New Jersey, and the deal was that graduates would be offered a job within a certain number of years or their remaining tuition bill would be canceled.

When she graduated, the employment market had shifted, and there were too many nurses for the available jobs. They did not have a job for her, and they canceled her tuition balance.

She found a job elsewhere within a reasonable time, and her life became enhanced because of a single idea of possibility. Thank You, God!

16 - Quotes For You

If you want to lift yourself up, lift up someone else.
- Booker T. Washington

You will never experience true freedom or riches unless you learn to think for yourself.
- Dr. Robert Anthony

17 - Can You Help Carry A Message

Be A Messenger of Better Options

Things You Can Do

1. Develop patience, understanding, and plant seeds to a crop of possibilities.

2. Study the laws and ask questions.

3. Google Prison Reform Topics on the internet and read up on all the efforts out there and support those that you agree with.

4. Help the legal representatives of the people to understand what works and what does not.

5. Be respectful of the efforts of others.

6. Read about the struggles of the Correctional Authorities and advise options that you can see but they cannot.

7. Help the families of those who are incarcerated.

8. Look out for and support the children of those who are in prison.

18 - Can You Help Community Service

Be A Community Service Angel
Things You Can Share To Improve Quality of Life

1. Teach Parents not to buy Toy Guns that can get their child killed by mistake. Toy Guns Are Obsolete.

2. Help Addicts have a Prayer and a chance at
http://AngelRaphaelSpeaks.com/Addicts-Prayer/

3. Help Alcoholics have a Prayer and a chance at
http://AngelRaphaelSpeaks.com/Alcoholics-Prayer/

4. Help People Prepare for Health Care Emergencies
http://angelraphaelspeaks.com/441-2/

5. Help Communicate & Save Lives with
http://AngelRaphaelSpeaks.com/English-Language-Helper-Template-for-Non-English-Speakers/

6. Help Bring Peace to Troubled people by sending them to
http://Create-A-Prayer.com

7. Help Reduce Stress at http://StressReleaseCoach.com

8. Help prisoners and their families find some peace at
http://AngelRaphaelSpeaks.com/Prisons/

19 - Can You Help Communication

Read and Advise Skills Needed

Things You Can Do Pro Bono

1. If you read any of my messages and you have an opinion, I would love to hear it.

2. If you read any of my messages and you have a clarification, I would love to hear it.

3. If you read any of my messages and you have an idea, I would love to hear it.

4. If you read any of my messages and you have an objection, I would love to hear it.

5. If you read any of my messages and you have a comment, I would love to hear it.

6. If you read any of my messages and you have a variation, I would love to hear it.

7. If you read any of my messages and you have any of the above, I would love for you to write about it elsewhere also.

Volunteer Editors Welcome

Volunteer Beta Readers Welcome

For
Considering
These
Ideas

Ever

It Does Not Help Prayer Still Does!

Resource: http://Create-A-Prayer.com

22 - Resource List

Distant Healing Sessions (or Join Mail List) – Write To mikewann@voicenet.com

Books by Rev. Mike at www.Amazon.com:

Veterans Healing Six Pack
1. *Trauma Healing Options for VA Hospitals: Help for Veterans to Own Their Healing and their future.*
2. *Trauma Healing Action Steps for Veterans: Help to Start Healing*
3. *Trauma Healing Action Steps for Veterans: Empowerment*
4. *Trauma Healing Action Steps for Veterans: Forgiveness*
5. *Trauma Healing Action Steps for Veterans: Thought Freedom*
6. *Tea for Veterans: Welcome One Home*

PTSD Power Pack:
1. *The PTSD Project: Turn Pain To Power*
2. *PTSD & Soul Retrieval: Putting One Back Together*
3. *PTSD & The Purple PAD: Calling all Scientists and PTSD Patients*

Angel Raphael Speaks Volume 1: Take Courage! God Has Healing in Store for You!
Angel Raphael Speaks Volume 2: Take Courage! God Has Healing in Store for You!
Angel Raphael Speaks Volume 3: Take Courage! God Has Healing in Store for You!
Angel Raphael Speaks Volume 4: Angels, Addicts, Alcoholics & Prisoners – Oh Yeah!
Angel Raphael Speaks Volume 5: Prisoners Caring for Alcoholics - Australia In Miniature Projects Intro
Angel Raphael Speaks Volume 6: Prisoners Caring for Addicts - Australia In Miniature For Addicts
Reiki Journaling from Japan
Reiki Is Alive: God's Great Gift
Four Parts to Healing
Distant Healing: We Are All Connected

Prison Reiki? Maybe Someday? A Gateway To Help Heal Prisons & America?
Judges and An Angel Rule On Possibilities: We Can Cut Sentences & Prison Costs
Ideas For Prison Wardens: Leadership Is Not Easy
Solitary Community: Could Community Support Cut Costs and Issues?
Prison Project Communications Team: Communications Can Change Lives
Motivating & Empowering Prisoners? Invite Prisoners To Find Their Motivation
Prison Segmentation For Safety, And Sanity, Security, Peace, and Space
Prison Segmentation For Security
Dowsing for Prisoners; Answers from Above
Ex-Prisoner Possibilities With Real Estate Investors
Prison Segmentation For Joint Ventures
Prison Segmentation For Your Rehabilitation: R U Ready?
Prison Segmentation For Family Villages
Prison Segmentation For Senior Prisoners
Prison Segmentation For Coaching Clubs
Prison Segmentation For Miracles
Prison Segmentation For A Prison Game Show
Prison Segmentation For Spousal Support
Prison Segmentation For Exit Contracts
Prison Segmentation For Sentence Segments
Penitentiary Edition Angel Raphael Speaks

Little Books on Kindle.com by Rev. Mike:
English Medical History Questionnaire For Non-English Speakers
English Language Helper For Non-English Speakers
Wise Wonderful Women Are The Well Of The Family
Answers to Test & Research: Dowsing Power
Crisis? Reiki! Baby? Reiki!
Bible References For Healing
Angel Raphael Speaks – Prisons
Angel Raphael Speaks – Veterans
The Saint Off Interstate 95

23 - Angels Please Prayers

Addict's

Angels of Healing Selected
Help Me to Stay Directed
Come To Me From The Sky
I Am Ready to Succeed Not Try
If I Don't Invite You In
I Might Not Win
I Have Been Lost For Too Long
Help Me To Stay Strong

&

Alcoholic's

Angels of Healing On High
Help Me to Stay Dry
Come To Me From The Sky
I Am Ready to Succeed Not Try
If I Don't Invite You In
I Might Not Win
I Have Been Lost For Too Long
Help Me To Stay Strong

From

ANGELS ARE ALWAYS
AROUND ADDICTS
AND ALCOHOLICS

HELP IS NEAR NOW!
INVITE IT IN!

REVEREND
MIKE WANNER

http://AngelRaphaelSpeaks.com/AAAAAAA/

24 - Private Channeling

Angel Raphael Speaks a series of free messages that are channeled through Reverend Mike Wanner for the Highest good and Highest Healing of all concerned.

Many questions arise about Reverend Mike doing private channeling, and he does help with that so e-mail him.

Reverend Mike is available worldwide as a psychic channel, emotional release facilitator, spiritual energy practitioner & teacher, and public speaker. He looks forward to meeting you soon!

Email - <u>mikewann@voicenet.com</u> 215-342-1270

PRIVATE SPIRITUAL READINGS/channelings or Spiritual Healing Sessions: Telephone or in person.

Rev. Mike is available for individual, intuitive one-on-one sessions with you, his Guide Family, and your Guides. He helps by offering clarity on emotional situations about your life, your purpose, your spirituality, and the release of stuffed emotions and cellular memory.

Connect to the love of your Guides today!

Contact Rev. Mike for an appointment.

Sessions available:

Spiritual Readings
Angel Channeling
Distant Reiki Healing
Distant Clearing of Stuffed Emotions
Distant Clearing Cellular Memory
Distant Clearing Energy Blockages
Distant Clearing of the Chakras
Customized needs
Mastermind dowsing responses to yes/no direction finding questions.

Rev. Mike is a facilitator of healing. He brings you and the Divine together so that you can align with the Divine and have a great time and a great life. All healing is between you and God, as it should be.

Go ahead and start without Rev. Mike. Visit his prayer site http://www.Create-A-Prayer.com. Take the first step NOW.

25 - Reverend Mike Wanner

Rev. Mike Wanner started his spiritual and ministerial studies with Reiki in 1993 and had studied seven styles of Reiki in the U.S., Japan, Canada, Denmark and Australia. He is certified to teach. He became certified to teach Integrated Energy Therapy in 1999 and co-taught the first IET class of the new Millennium. Mike began dowsing in 2001.

Ordained as a Metaphysical Minister of the International Metaphysical Ministry and an Interfaith Minister of the Circle of Miracles Ministry, Rev. Mike practices and teaches spiritual energy therapies in the Philadelphia Area.

Rev. Mike holds ministerial degrees from the University of Metaphysics and the University of Sedona. He is a Pastoral Care Associate at Jefferson - Aria - Frankford Hospital. He taught at the National Academy of Massage Therapy and Health Sciences.

Rev. Mike was a faculty member of the Medical Mission Sister's Center for Human Integration's School of Integrated Body/Mind Therapies in Fox Chase, Philadelphia, PA for twelve years.

Rev. Mike is licensed by the teaching of Intuitional Metaphysics to practice Spiritual Healing and Scientific Prayer. Mike is also a Prayer therapist.

Rev. Mike was elected in 2007 to the status of "Fellow of the American Institute of Stress."

In 2008, Rev. Mike became a practitioner of Coincidental Recognition as he incorporated the CoRe system into his spiritual healing practice.

In 2009, Rev. Mike trademarked a new healing process called Quantum Quatro! Subtle Energy System Support®.
In 2011, Rev. Mike joined the outreach program known as the Health Advantage Group.

In 2012, Rev. Mike became a Certified Professional Coach by The Master Coaching Academy and Joined The Personal Empowerment Group.

Prior to his spiritual, ministerial and coaching studies, Rev. Mike worked for Sears Roebuck and Co. while in High School and after graduation, until he joined the U. S. Air Force in 1965. He returned to Sears from Vietnam in 1969 and stayed until 1978. His final Sears assignment was as an efficiency expert in Methods - Operational Research and Development.

He volunteered with Burholme Emergency Medical Services from 1969 and is still a Life Member and Board of Directors Member. He started a private ambulance company in 1975 and worked professionally in the field until 2001 when he devoted his full attention to real estate investing, healing, coaching, and writing.

www.ReverendMikeWanner.com

www.ingramcontent.com/pod-product-compliance
Lightning Source LLC
Chambersburg PA
CBHW071158220526
45468CB00003B/1075